THE
LEAD
THROUGH
METHOD

THE
LEAD
THROUGH
METHOD

THE PROVEN STEPS TO GETTING UNSTUCK, LEADING YOUR LIFE, AND GETTING RESULTS.

FORMER UNITED STATES SECRET SERVICE OFFICER

JOSE VARGAS

V
Enterprise
Jose Vargas

TABLE OF CONTENTS

"If you are willing to do what others won't do, you will have an influence others won't have."

Craig Groeschel

INTRODUCTION

When I was in the sixth grade, I experienced my first indoor rock climbing experience. I was as excited as any pre-teen boy would be to show his wild side. Climbing that wall would show the world who's boss! I was strapped into a harness that looked like underwear over my jeans. With a rope tied to it, I felt secure and safe, so up I went. With one hand and one foot climbing together, I made my way up. My gaze was focused and I kept going until I finally reached the top of what seemed to be a twenty foot high wall.

What happened next was unplanned. Upon reaching the top, I felt a rush of fear flooding my body. My terrorized thoughts were inundated with "What if I fall?" and "This is so high!" and "How in the world am I going to get back down?" The ground now seemed

11

200 feet below, and I felt sick to my stomach, totally frozen in place.

At that same moment, the person in charge yelled, "Okay, you can come back down now!" But I was paralyzed. I held on tightly for dear life to the top of that wall. Tears welled up, and then came embarrassment. The longer I was there, more people crowded below to look up at me, encouraging me to come down. But it wasn't encouraging! It wasn't helping! Then, I noticed a very big man with a heavy beard climbing up the wall toward me. As he approached me, he didn't shame me or criticize me. He gently whispered, "I am here with you, and I will help you get down. Just hold on to me. You will be okay." Shaking, I nodded, clung to him, and down we went. Safe on the ground again! After that experience, I didn't go rock climbing for a very long time. So much for showing the world who was boss!

What's the point of this story? First, most people get stuck at some point in their lives and need someone who will help them get free. More importantly, if you want to get breakthroughs and get unstuck, you have to take ownership of your life. This book will help you gain confidence and clarity so that you can be a leader and make the impact you desire. Most likely, you are not currently fearful on the top of a wall, but you may be experiencing some challenging moments. These moments may have left you feeling stuck, unsure, or even paralyzed with fear. You were doing great, having some successes, yet now you feel stuck, ashamed, and afraid.

Here is the second lesson. My rescuer gave me his courage. He gave me hope. He offered help from a place of safety and confidence. Just as that man helped me down, that's what we as leaders desire to do for others. That's the point of this book. I want to give you my hand in the form of a method I have used many times in my career and in my life.

The third lesson in this story that I would like to re-iterate to you is this: although that man came to rescue a frightened child, let me be the first to tell you, no one is coming to "rescue" you. You are going to have to lead yourself out, or through, whatever obstacle, challenge, or situation in which you might find your-self. You can't, and should not, wait for someone to come, because they just may not be coming. You need to rise up and be the leader of your life. The fact that you are reading this book is a step in that direction. You are taking ownership of your life and leadership.

I have interacted with countless people with so much potential who have been stuck on their own walls, whether in jobs they hated, health they ne-glected, finances they ignored, relationships they tol-erated, or faith that was almost non-existent. I have witnessed how fear has robbed so much from so many potential leaders. It has robbed them of untapped potential, amazing opportunities, and fulfillment. I have seen how these men and women are stuck in life, desperately wanting to change their circumstances, but they are not clear on how to proceed. So, they do nothing, or keep doing the same things that do not give them the results they desire.

The reason I wrote this book is because I have been there as well. I have been through jobs I hated, health I neglected, and with finances I didn't understand. Yet, early in my life, I was fortunate to realize that if I was going to see things change and improve, and not repeat the mistakes of past generations, then I had to take charge. If I was going to get breakthroughs and see the results in all areas of my life, I was going to have to lead my life instead of just drifting and hoping things would change for me.

I realize that there are some things you must learn to manage while you build the life you desire, but if you don't move forward wisely, then nothing will change. You will always remain stuck. I have proceeded to pursue my dreams, goals, and passions with intensity and intentionality, by digesting books, watching documentaries, and studying the lives of successful leaders who have had their own breakthrough moments. Because of it, I am living what I call a LeadThrough life, and I believe the same can be true for you.

What is the LeadThrough life? It is when you lead your life towards the breakthroughs you desire, get unstuck, and pursue the path to impact results and fulfillment. If something is not working in your life right now, you have the power to change it. If your faith is not as deep as you want it to be, you can deepen it. If you have a desire to change, grow, and see results in your personal and professional life, then this book is for you. You are the leader of your life. You have to be the one to take ownership and choose to **get unstuck and onto the path to results, impact, and fulfillment.**

I will share the steps I took every time I have been stuck. These steps have allowed me to marry the love of my life and to fulfill one of my long dreams of becoming a United States Secret Service Officer. These steps have helped me to persevere through obstacles and overcome many challenges. I will share with you some of my story with the hope that you too will see the amazing leader you can be.

NO SHAME

First things first, there is no shame in getting stuck in life. *Everyone has mountains to climb up and mountains to climb down.* The fact is, everyone has been stuck. Every great leader has been through moments when they've questioned themselves, have been dis-satisfied with where they are, or have been stuck in despair or hopelessness. These are the same individuals who have inspired us to climb higher, to be bold, and to persevere through setbacks and challenges. Being stuck can simply be not knowing the next step that you need to take, personally or professionally.

I want to show you how you can lead your life, see breakthroughs, and get the results you desire in every area of your life. I believe that every area of your life, personally and professionally, is interconnected and each affects the other. You don't have to be without hope. You don't have to put up a false front. You can implement the practical steps that I have outlined in this book to get your breakthroughs. You don't have to just accept your life as it is, but you can lead your life towards excellence and with impact. Face it, isn't that what you want? You want to have impact in this world, and you want to have impact with the people in your life. So, let's get started.

CHAPTER 1

TIME TO GET UNSTUCK

*"It does not matter how slowly you
go as long as you do not stop."*
Confucius

What if you didn't have to settle for where you are? What if there is a better vision for your life? I wrote this book in part because I believe there is. But you must lead yourself towards that life and follow that vision. Leaders are visionaries. They don't just look at the present as it is; they look to the future, at how things could be. In this book, you will look at your life as it is, but I will also challenge you to examine your life as it could be.

As I went into the Oval Office for the first time, I felt awe and an overwhelming sense of reverence. I thought about all the great individuals who have led our country from that place. Every president from

John Adams to President Trump—in the room where I was now standing. As I looked up, I saw the United States Presidential Seal engraved in the ceiling. I could hardly believe I was really there. Yet, I was, and not as a tourist, but as a protector of The President of the United States of America. In a rush of emotions, I thought about men like Martin Luther King Jr. who came to that very place to share his vision of equality for Americans and for the world. As I looked around, I saw the desk that President John F. Kennedy had used. President Kennedy had challenged Americans to do something that was going to supersede the present. It was going to be an achievement for the entire world.

In a speech in Texas, Kennedy had given a history lesson on the advancements of mankind. He had issued a bold and challenging vision of the future, particularly sending a man to the moon to explore space for the first time. *"No space ships, technology wasn't there. No one has ever done it before, there are innumerable risks."* Kennedy understood, *"The high cost will give us high reward,"* and then he went on to quote William Bradford from the 1630s. Bradford was among the passengers on the Mayflower's trans-Atlantic journey, and upon arriving in Massachusetts in 1620, he had signed the Mayflower Compact[1].

"All great and honorable actions are accompanied with

great difficulties and both must be enterprise and over-come with answerable courage," Kennedy continued. And then, he went on to say, *"We choose to go to the moon, not because it is easy, but because it is hard."* Kennedy understood that leaders always go first and they always are willing to make the hard decisions. They don't wait, sit on the sidelines, and hope for things to happen. As a matter of fact, he said, *"The greater our knowledge increases, the greater our ignorance unfolds."* He defied logic at that time but challenged the odds, the nay-sayers, and the people who wanted to wait. I believe that you are reading this book because you would like to do the same thing in your own personal and professional life.

You chose this book because you have a goal you want to accomplish in life, a breakthrough you must walk through. Kennedy's breakthrough moment was to put a man on the moon. Your breakthrough moment is perhaps to become a better man or woman at home or at the office, or to reach financial independence, or to triple your company's profits this year, or to streamline your product to multiple retailers, or to increase your volunteers and donations from your non-profit organization. Perhaps your goal is to send your kids to college, pay off debt, lose thirty extra pounds, or you want to lead well and impact lives.

The goal is different for each of us, but anytime you are going into new territories or new levels, it's going to take innovation, creativity, risk, planning, faith, hope, perseverance, and most of all, it's going to take self-leadership to help you get your breakthroughs.

What is the LeadThrough Method, and how do you live a LeadThrough life? The LeadThrough Method is when you lead your life towards the breakthroughs you desire, get unstuck, and be on the path to results, impact, and fulfillment.

The LeadThrough Method is a culmination of steps that I have taken over the last fifteen plus years in my own life and in the lives of the people and organizations that I have been able to lead. It is the method that will help you go from a bystander of life's circumstances to an intentional leader moving towards your goals, and it will give you the tools to create a lasting impact on those around you. This method will increase your joy and fulfillment, and it will activate personal growth. It is one of the methods for achieving the success you desire for your life, professionally and personally.

LEADTHROUGH

LeadThrough is a combination of two powerful words broken up and stitched together— leadership and breakthrough. These two words have resonated within me for years. I have been stuck in jobs I wasn't passionate about, experienced painful personal situations, encountered tough leadership decisions, and dealt with challenging circumstances that I have had to manage. Yet, these two words have allowed me to not only come out from being stuck but to thrive in my journey. This method is what will help get you, like President Kennedy, to your own "moon exploration." Although President Kennedy never saw it in his lifetime, I want you to see it in yours. It is what will allow you to experience a new level of success. **These are the following steps on your path to results, impact, and fulfilling your biggest desires.**

STEP 1–LOCATE IT

Articulate your current situation as it is today. You can't get to where you need to go until you become aware of where you are. In this step, you will answer the question: "Where are you?" As you complete the other steps in this method, you will understand why this step is foundational and how this step will revolutionize the way you think about yourself.

STEP 2–DISSECT IT

You did not get to step one without leaving clues for yourself as to how you got there. To understand where you are, you have to answer the question: "What has led you to where you are?" Dissecting means to cut open, to understand from within. In this step, you will take the time to break down and uncover the reasons behind your successes and failures. This awareness will prevent you from repeating mistakes, and it will provide feedback to accelerate your progress.

STEP 3—DREAM IT

After understanding your location and how you got there, now the fun begins. In this step, you will answer the question: "What do you want?" This is the step where you stop dwelling on your yesterdays and you look ahead to where you want to go. Dream big, and be specific enough in this step, considering every area of your life or business, in order to clarify what you want or need for the journey.

STEP 4—DEFINE IT

"Why do you want it?" Not only must you know what you want, but you must also answer the question of why you want it. Motivation is important to obtaining what you want. The worst thing is to climb a ladder only to discover that you had it leaning on the wrong wall. Discovering your true motives will fuel you to pursue the right things, not just the good things. It will keep you focused.

STEP 5—PLAN IT

You can have passion, and you can have talent, but without a plan, your dream and goals will soon turn into frustration. Knowing what you want is half the battle; understanding why you want it is another, but creating a plan is what will almost ensure you get there! "What do you need to do to get there?" This is the step to work out your plan as far as you can see it.

STEP 6—PAY IT

Not only do we often fail to count the cost of what it will take to get what we want, but many times, we don't settle in our hearts if we will pay the price necessary to win. What challenges will you confront on your way to where you want to go? "Are you willing to pay the price?" Now is the time to think about this battle.

STEP 7—MAKE IT

Planning is important, and being willing to pay the price necessary to get what you want is critical. However, without action behind your desires, nothing will happen. What action steps will you take in order to overcome the challenges and objections towards your goal? Ask yourself: " How will you stay motivated on the journey?"

> *"If you talk about it, it's a dream. If you envision it, it's possible, but if you schedule it, it's real."*
> Tony Robbins

There is more for you.
Let's get to work!

Dr. John Delony is a successful professional in counseling. He has a PHD in higher education and loves to help people. He is a leading voice on relationships and mental health across America. He is also a Ramsey Solutions Personality and host of The Dr. John Delony Show, where he guides callers through real life mental health challenges and relationship issues. But prior to this, Dr. Delony was a very successful senior leader at multiple universities. In addition, he is a father and husband. He was climbing the corporate ladder and making a lot of money when something happened in his life that stalled his progress. He shared in his book *Redefining Anxiety*, "*I was living the dream, but I couldn't shake this feeling that I was malfunctioning. That I was breaking apart in my own skin. I am losing my mind and I need help.*" Dr. Delony found himself struggling with anxiety and was overwhelmed[2].

As I reflected on this, I was able to understand

the concept of his book in practice. This is the moment where perhaps he felt "stuck," but his story doesn't end there. Dr. Delony began to search for answers. He began to take steps in what I call the LeadThrough Method. He identified where he was and his current reality. He addressed what he was feeling, and with help, he figured out how he got there. Dr. Delony also knew where he wanted to be, and he created a plan for what it would take to get there. He sought out doctors, mentors, counselors, and friends for wisdom, and he ultimately bounced back stronger and better. Now, he serves millions of people who listen to his show and read about his work. Dr. Delony's story is encouraging and a perfect example of how you can apply these principles in your own life and journey.

As you go through the questions outlined in this book and begin to answer them, the answers will bring awareness to your current reality with no pretense or filters. This awareness will lead you to have clarity, and once you are clear to see the next step, then you will have the courage and confidence to move towards your desired results.

CONFRONTING + REALITY = AWARENESS
AWARENESS = CLARITY
CLARITY = COURAGE

Throughout this book, you will answer each question for every step. I will be referring to your personal and professional life, which are outlined below.

PERSONAL LIFE	+	PROFESSIONAL LIFE
↓		↓
Mental		Career
Physical		Working Relationships
Emotional		Goals
Relational		Growth
Financial		
Spiritual		

When you get stuck in your professional or personal life, it might feel like you are hitting roadblocks and obstacles. You will always have a choice. You can settle for where you are, choose to retreat to where you came from, or you can choose to grow as you proceed in life. Many people throw their hands in the air and give up trying to become better. They choose to settle because the process of growth requires leadership. I am sure you picked up this book because you want to lead your life. But here is what I want you to know: Leadership is hard! The hardest person you will ever lead is yourself. Leadership is going first and allowing others to get the benefits of what has cost you trial and error.

28

Leadership is living life in such a way that reflects love, inspires change, and calls for action.

It starts with self. It's hard, but so is choosing to stay where you are. Any difficulty you encounter is the price of choosing not to settle, choosing to be more, and choosing to live life to the fullest. Dr. Delony could have coasted by pretending that nothing was happening. Internally, he could have said, *"I am successful, no need to panic, no need to change."* But he paid attention to the tension, to where he really was internally, and knew that he couldn't remain there. He needed to go forward in life. I am grateful he chose to lead himself. Now he leads a massive amount of people across America and around the world through hardships and confusion.

It's possible for you as well.

You must understand that there is more for you. You can overcome your obstacles, challenges, or mindset. But first, you must understand this reality:

It's okay to be stuck at times.

Big wins and deep losses can often bring extreme emotions. Emotions such as fear, doubt, shame, worry, and anxiety. These emotions tend to drive us in a certain direction. Think of the story of my wall climbing experience. I was stuck there, paralyzed by fear on top of the wall, and the longer I stayed up there, the more shame I felt. But here is the reality: It didn't start out that way. I was excited to climb that wall! It was a great new adventure! Yet, I allowed thoughts to penetrate my mind to the point it caused fear that permeated throughout my body and froze me on my tracks. The same is true for you. You have a vision of what you want for your life or for what your organization should look like, yet something happened that stopped you.

The COVID-19 global pandemic is an example. There is so much uncertainty about it in the world, in the job market, and even in our own lives. There have been many major changes and we often feel as if we have no control. This feeling can often lead us to spiral out of control. How can you have a degree of control while everything seems to be out of your control? As you lead your life towards fulfillment and impact, you must control what you can, and give yourself some grace for those areas you can't control.

You alone cannot control the market, the weather, the decisions of others, or even those closest to you. Yes, you can influence, but you can't control. Thinking you could will cause frustration and disappointment. But there is good news! Here is what you can control. You can control how you think and even talk to yourself during hard moments. You can control what you watch on television or what you scroll on social media. You can choose what to pick up and read. You can choose to listen to something that will build you up, instill faith, or that will dispel fear. You can control what you eat and how you take care of your body by exercising regularly. You choose how you display love to the people in your life. You have some control over those areas. You can control how you view the people who are looking to you for leadership, whether it be your family or your team. You can control what you model to them with how you lead, love, and serve them. When you focus on what you can control in your own life, then these feelings that try to paralyze you will begin to dissipate, unleashing the greatness within you.

"If you are always trying to be normal, you will never know how amazing you can be."

Maya Angelou

QUESTIONS & REFLECTION

CHAPTER 2

TAKE THE PILL

"If we are going to lead well, we must dissect both failure and success."

Jose Vargas

Before we dive into the actual steps you need to take to get a breakthrough and live a LeadThrough life, let me help you prepare your mind and heart for the journey. So, in this chapter, I want you to take a pill.

What if I told you there was a pill that, if you took it, would develop all the strengths and qualities you need to begin this breakthrough process? What if that pill allowed you to accomplish your goals? Perhaps you want to be a better father, husband, or a better employee or better leader. I want to offer you that pill. Like the movie "The Matrix," I extend my hand now. It's not narcotics. You don't need a prescription. It's not blue or red. It doesn't even have negative side effects.

This pill is a series of disciplines that, if you apply daily, and combine them with the method that you will learn in the upcoming pages, it will compound into a ripple effect of change and transformation in your life and to those around you.

The word PILL is an acronym:

P–Perseverance
I–Intentionality
L–Learning
L–Leadership

For years, I have struggled with severe migraines. Often, these migraines have had me rushing to the Emergency Room because of the excruciating pain. One day, as I was in the ER, the doctors gave me what they called a cocktail of medicine to treat the pain. This cocktail was so helpful that it was the first time my pain was relieved so quickly, within seconds. Now, I appreciate medicine, especially if I am having a severe migraine. But the cocktail of medication is temporary. I don't like taking medicine. There are side effects, and it's just not the best for me.

This pill I am prescribing for you is different. If you put into action these disciplines, it will give you the desired outcome you want in your life and leadership. Let's now look at the first word.

Perseverance is a skill and an attitude that you can develop and must possess, because in life, if you haven't figured it out by now, you will go through tough challenges, obstacles, and hard situations. These challenges tempt you to want to quit, give up, or throw in the towel, but you will have to refuse that urge to give up. Sometimes you will feel resistance as you choose to grow and to move forward. Quite frankly, people who never experience resistance are people who are sitting on the sideline of life. But as a leader, someone who decided to lead their life and live a LeadThrough life, you have gotten in the game, you are in the arena, and regardless of what happens, ***don't quit***. Theodore Roosevelt once said, *"It is not the critic who counts; not the man who points out how the strong man stumbles, or where the doer of deeds could have done them better. The credit belongs to the man who is actually in the arena, whose face is marred by dust and sweat and blood; who strives valiantly; who errs, who comes short again and again, because there is no effort without error and shortcoming; but who does actually strive to do the deeds; who knows great enthusiasms, the great devotions; who spends himself in a worthy cause; who at the best knows in the end the triumph of high achievement, and who at the worst, if he fails, at least fails while daring greatly, so that his place shall never be with those cold and timid souls who neither know victory nor defeat."*

A LeadThrough life requires "doses" of perseverance. As you begin your journey to get unstuck, you will need to be reminded of this truth. Leaders who demonstrate perseverance give us hope. They give us courage, and they help us press on when we feel like giving up. They persevere because they know that what they are after is far greater than what they currently have. You are on your way there as well.

The next "ingredient" in the PILL is the word Intentionality.

Intentionality—A LeadThrough life requires you to be intentional every step of the way. You need to be intentional about your thoughts, to be careful to observe and filter what you feed your mind by what you watch and listen to on a **daily basis**. You must also be intentional about what you do on a *daily basis*, remembering that your actions will ultimately create your life. No one wakes up one day being great at what they do. It takes work, day in and day out. It will also take work and intentionality to get your breakthrough.

Many people struggle with this particular discipline. They think success is found in the high "mountains of life." But success is found in the everyday, seemingly insignificant things. How you make decisions each day will dictate how far you will go in life. Become intentional in how you respond at work. How do you perform at your job when no one is watching? How do you speak to yourself while driving home from the office? How do you treat your team or, better yet, those closest to you, including your family? Being intentional in all of these areas is critical to achieve the success you need, to not only look good on the outside and on your favorite social media channel, but to actually be fulfilled in your soul as you are accomplishing your goals and becoming a leader worth following. Everything you do has to be intentional.

Notice, I didn't say perfect. No one is. Leadership expert John C. Maxwell said it best in his book, *Intentional Living*: *"When you live each day with intentionality, there's almost no limit to what you can do. You can transform yourself, your family, your community, and your nation. When enough people do that, they can change the world. When you intentionally use your everyday life to bring about positive change in the lives of others, you begin to live a life that matters."* Leading a life of breakthroughs, a life you are proud of, is created by being intentional. When you fall short, you intentionally rise up again and strive to be better next time. On your journey, choose to be intentional in your thoughts, your words, and your actions. The next ingredient in the PILL is the word Leadership.

Leadership is one of my favorite words. I believe our lives will get better and our organizations will thrive when we decide to lead them. When we get better as leaders, our families will get better, and our situations will improve. When we develop as leaders, our businesses thrive, and so do the people in our care. People around us are better because of us. I truly believe that leadership is the key to transforming your life and profession. You have to decide each day to lead yourself first and then lead those who choose to follow.

I have read many definitions of leadership over the past fifteen years. I have worked for leaders, been involved in leadership roles, and I agree with John C. Maxwell, who defines leadership as the following: "*Leadership is influence, nothing more and nothing less.*" The ability to influence another human being is a powerful concept. The ability to guide people in a direction is something we shouldn't take lightly. *My definition of leadership is living life in such a way that reflects love, inspires change, and calls for action.*

Look at your life, starting with your family, then move into your job or career, then into your community, your church, your circles. Are you living in such a way that you are reflecting love towards those with whom you come in contact? Are you living in such a way that those in your circle are inspired to change and actually take steps to change the course of their lives? Perhaps something you have said allowed them to see hope in their own relationships, or finances, business, or faith. You can have that power. This is why developing your leadership ability is critical in getting breakthroughs and leading your life forward in the direction you desire.

Becoming a better leader is far greater than just reading all the books, going to all the classes, and attending every workshop. Leadership is understanding that you can get better daily and inspire those around you to do the same. The reality is that you as a person are constantly changing, either intentionally, in the direction that you want, or passively by your life's circumstances. I have come to the conclusion that it is leaders who understand that because life is ever changing, we must change with it. You must be intentional about growing and developing yourself as a leader. There is so much to learn about yourself and others. Therefore, there is so much to learn about leadership, which brings us to the last word in the PILL acronym, Learning.

Learning- Why are we attracted and motivated by leaders who are on the move; leaders who are building something, or doing something of significance? Why are we inspired by those who are always pushing the limits? When I think about this, I think about Amazon founder, Jeff Bezos. Years ago, he had a dream and started selling books online, and he has since turned that little store into an empire that is worth billions of dollars today. Amazon has employed thousands of people and has served millions of people. I was marveled and amazed as I watched him go into space through the creation of his own company, Blue Origin. Regardless of whether you like him or not, doesn't that inspire you? Why do we lean forward when we hear stories of discovery, triumph, and victory? I believe we are attracted to this type of living, because we are hardwired by our Creator to grow, to learn, to be curious, and to constantly be asking, "Why?" If I tell my daughter Evie not to touch the cookie jar, she most likely will. This quest for adventure, for discovery, is embedded inside of us.

Becoming a student again is the key to constantly growing. We must not allow our successes, positions, or titles make us believe that we somehow have arrived. I love what the New Testament Apostle Paul said: *"Brothers, I do not consider that I have made it my own. But one thing I do: forgetting what lies behind and straining forward to what lies ahead,"* (Philippians 3:13 ESV)[1]. Remembering what you learned yesterday is a must, but remembering yesterday should help you lead better today. Learning is being able to receive and accept feedback. Some people run from this. They get offended or fire people who dare give feedback. I love what someone once said: *"If you push back from feedback, you push back from a better version of yourself."*

A LeadThrough life will demand that you continue to grow, to look at what lies ahead and stretch towards it. These leaders I've mentioned earlier, along with Paul, never stopped learning, and therefore, they never stopped growing. Stay engaged in life by staying inquisitive, asking questions, and getting around others who are ahead of you in some areas of life. What does it take to be this way? One of my beliefs is that I can learn anything. As long as I am interested and have a strong desire for it, I will learn. I believe that to be true of you as well.

I remember not enjoying reading books or studying while I was growing up. As a matter of fact, I really didn't like school. After high school, though, I was leading a group of young people at my church. One day while driving, I had an epiphany. I remember hearing in my heart, *"If you are going to lead people, you are going to have to grow yourself."* That was the moment I became a student. That was the moment that began the shift in my life. At first, I was struggling to read. I didn't retain what I read, but I kept doing it everyday. Shortly after, I noticed my language improving, my ideas were bigger, and my world view was amplifying. As a person of faith, my Bible was coming alive! The more I learned, the more I realized how much more there is to learn. I was hooked, and now, I love learning! It's part of who I am. But most importantly, I am constantly growing. The reason I share this story with you is to encourage you to throw away the excuses that you can't learn or retain information, or that learning simply something you don't like. You can teach yourself to love it, and you can learn to do that in this book.

Just think about high school or college. You may not have enjoyed your classes, but you endured them so that you could graduate. Well, life is like that, but it's not meant to be endured. You are meant to learn, enjoy, grow, and lead your life towards the vision you have been given.

One final component in learning is being and staying humble. No one wants to follow someone who has been teaching lessons and doing the same things from five or ten years ago. Stay fresh, find new perspectives, find stories that inspire you and challenge you to grow as you challenge those you lead. Remember, passion is contagious. Plus, if you choose not to learn and grow, you will no longer be leading, you will be settling.

"Learning without thought is labor lost;
thought without learning is perilous."

Confucius

So, now that you understand the PILL, I hope you take a dose of it everyday. The attributes in the PILL acronym must be developed. It's actually the only way to acquire these qualities. No one can hand them to you, buy them for you, wrap them up, and give them to you. You have to develop them. That's good news because it means you are in control. You don't have to wait for someone to come alongside you and hope they inspire you. You must move and find it yourself. Seek and you will find. You have to put in the work. Every single day. No one drifts towards success. No one accidentally becomes a successful leader. You have to be intentional about taking life and the aspects you can control and lead them. That's how you get breakthroughs.

I grew up without my father in my life, and one of the desires that I had when my first daughter, Evie, was born, is that I was going to be intentional about being involved in her life. Every aspect of it. I was committed to changing diapers. I was going to wake up in the middle of the night. I was going to feed her and burp her. My vision as a father is that one day, when my daughter is a woman, I want her to come home to visit often and put her arm around my shoulder and look me in the eyes and say, *"Dad, I love you so much, and you are my hero. Thank you for teaching me."* That may sound cheesy to you, but that is my vision for my fathering. Now that you know the recipe, or the PILL, to accelerate your leadership and are willing to take this PILL daily, you have positioned yourself to a LeadThrough life. Now read on, take the next steps of action, and get ready to get unstuck.

QUESTIONS & REFLECTION

CHAPTER 3

LOCATE IT

"You Will Know The Truth And The
Truth Will Set You Free."

Jesus of Nazareth

The first step to getting unstuck is what I call LOCATE IT. In this chapter, you will examine your current situation. This is your present reality but certainly not your permanent state. You can't get to where you are going until you become aware of where you are.

Have you ever been on a road trip and realized lunchtime was approaching, and you were craving a certain kind of food and you couldn't get it off your mind? You could almost taste it! You opened your phone's map or navigation system to find the nearest restaurant so you could quickly get your hands on that delicious meal you were craving. As you opened your map application on your phone, the first thing the app did was track your current location before it could guide you to your destination. Got that? It first had to locate you before it could tell you where you needed to go. That is what we will do to start your journey. To get your breakthrough and the results you desire, you first have to identify where you are, both professionally and personally.

Let me share with you a personal story. After finishing high school, I didn't have much direction, but I had some goals I wanted to accomplish. I wanted to be a speaker and communicator. I was intrigued with how communicators impacted their listeners by the words they spoke and how those words had the potential to redirect people's lives. I wanted to impact people in the same way. Shortly after realizing that desire, I had a few opportunities to speak in front of groups. I loved it! I knew this was one thing I was called to do. I also wanted to communicate through writing good books. I knew that books would outlive me, and I would be able to reach people I would never meet in person. So, imagine how I felt when I found out that my book, *The Detour*, had readers in Mexico, Canada, and even Egypt. I was blown away! I knew then that I could write about my experiences and lessons I had learned along the way, and it would help others.

Another goal I had was to have my own business. I didn't know what kind of business I wanted to have, but I wanted to use my skills and gifts to serve and help others. I also wanted to create an income that wasn't reliant on one source. I am now able to use my abilities to communicate and speak at various companies and non-profit organizations and earn income doing it. In addition, another goal I had was to become a police officer. I wanted to chase bad guys, help people, and impact lives in some meaningful way. I wanted to protect and save individuals, which meant carrying a gun and wearing a badge. How cool is that?

Shortly after high school, I proceeded to do just that. I took the Civil Service Police Test for Trenton, New Jersey, the city where I had spent my early childhood. I passed the test, but unfortunately, I didn't make it high enough on the list to allow me to attend the police academy. However, some years later, I repeated the process and made it. I received a letter of acceptance in the mail. I had a start date for the academy! My persistence had paid off. I remember wearing the boots and making sure they were very shiny prior to starting day one of my future life.

I could hardly believe it! I was excited and ready to go! I was there, wearing my boots and living my dream. I was doing the sit ups, jumping jacks, and hearing others get yelled at by the trainer. In the middle of a push up, a captain came to me and said, *"Recruit Vargas, come with me. Unfortunately, we won't be able to allow you to continue because the doctor would not clear you."* In reviewing my physical, they had found Wolff-Parkinson Syndrome (WPW) in my heart. I was crushed.

WPW is a type of congenital heart condition that causes a rapid heart rate. If you have WPW, you may have episodes of palpitations or rapid heartbeats. WPW affects less than one in one hundred people, and I had it. Normally, electrical signals travel through your heart in an organized way to control your heartbeat. This allows blood to pass from the upper chambers of your heart to the lower chambers and then travel throughout your body. These chambers are normally connected by a single main circuit in the center of the heart through which electricity flows. In WPW, there is an extra connection between the upper and lower chambers that can make you susceptible to arrhythmias causing rapid heart rates. (Tachycardia)[1].

In other words, I was a liability instead of an asset. They were afraid I would pass out in the middle of a chase or altercation and, as you can imagine, that wouldn't be so good. I wasn't able to continue at the academy, and my dream was crushed. The condition was found through an electrocardiogram done during my medical screening prior to starting the training.

Somehow, I missed the report and found out on day one of the class.

I went home that day and I was devastated, feeling like a balloon that was being elevated with helium and suddenly deflated. I was so discouraged. If you have ever had a dream snatched from you, you can imagine the devastation I felt. I went to bed that night wondering how this could have happened to me.

If you have ever tried to reach for something greater in life, whether personally or in business, you may go through moments of devastation and discouragement. But I want to warn you that if you ever desire to get a breakthrough to reach your goals, you have to shift your perspective.

After finding out what had happened, well-meaning friends said to me, "Maybe it just wasn't meant for you," and "Maybe you should move on," and "Maybe they were right." But I knew I wanted this, and I wasn't going to give up so easily. Besides, what mattered wasn't so much their perspective, or their thoughts—it was mine. What matters today is your perspective. You may not be able to change your situation overnight, but remember, even though you can't control most things in life, you can certainly change your perception of them.

Someone once said, *"Perspective is the way individuals see the world. It comes from their personal point of view and is shaped by life experiences, values, their current state of mind, the assumptions they bring into a situation and a whole lot of other things."*

Changing the way you view your situation is critical in getting your breakthrough. You can change your perspective by leading yourself to think clearly in a situation. To do that, start by asking and answering important questions. If you find yourself stuck in a situation, I want you to answer the following question:

Where are you?

The question may seem elementary, but it's loaded. Answering this question is critical. It is probably the most ancient question ever asked. In the Bible, this is the same question that God asked Adam and Eve in the beginning of time when they disobeyed God's command, ate from the forbidden fruit, and hid from God. In God's quest for them, He asked, *"Adam, where are you?"*

What a powerful question! This question forces you to confront the situation you are currently facing. It gives you clarity on what is really happening. It dispels the fog of confusion and illuminates the facts of where you are. It gives you personal and situational awareness. Again, you can't get to your destination without first tracking your current location. Answering this question makes you confront reality instead of hiding or neglecting your current state. You will then have a clear picture, not of what someone else said, but of what you are currently experiencing. This is your starting point. Someone once said, *"You can't get to where you are going until you understand where you've been."*

So, let's unpack this.

As you answer the question, "Where are you?" you can get unstuck and start seeing better results personally or professionally. The terms below will help you get started.

WHERE ARE YOU -

- **Geographically-** Do you like where you are living? Do you like the house or apartment in which you live? Do you like the neighborhood? What about the state or even the country?

- **Emotionally and Mentally-** How do you feel? What lies are you believing about yourself or your current situation? What stories do you continue to relive in your mind? Do you keep talking to yourself when no one is around?

- **Physically-** Are you in good health? Are you struggling to maintain your health?

- **Relationally-** What are the states of your

relationships, personally and professionally? Do you have friends in which you can confide? Does your family support what you are doing?

- **Career-** Are you in a career or job that you enjoy? Is there room for growth and progress there? Do you dread going to work? How are your coworkers? Do you have a good working relationship with your boss or supervisor?

- **Financially-** Are you able to support yourself financially? Is the financial state of your home or organization a good one? Do you have debt? Are you always thinking about money?

These are just some examples of how you can begin to unpack this question in your life and leadership. I want you to answer this question, "Where are you?" especially in the area that you need to obtain your desired results, in the area where you feel the most stuck. As you answer this question, pay attention to how you feel answering it. Awareness is one of the first keys to effectiveness, breakthrough, and good results.

As you are answering this question, you are turning on your own "GPS tracker," so to speak, so that you can identify your current location. Once you know where you are located, then you can be redirected to the next step to your destination.

THE DANGER EVERY LEADER FACES

As you locate where you are, remember that this is your starting point, not your destination. Beware of the following dangers you could face as you begin to unpack this truth.

In 2020, the year the world shut down due to a global pandemic, during the holidays, my wife and I knew we wanted to do certain activities that could lift our spirits and create lasting memories. One thing on her list was to watch *It's a Wonderful Life,* a sixty-plus -year-old movie. Did I mention it is in black and white? I tried to get her to change her mind about it. Did I mention, I don't like old movies? She insisted, and we ended up watching it. To my surprise, I loved it!

The main character was a man by the name of George Bailey. The movie portrayed heaven and angels, and one of the major angels assigned one of the minor angels, who needed to earn it's wings, to go to earth to help George Bailey. George was experiencing a critical moment in his life. He was going through something worse than an accident, worse than a disease, worse than poverty. George was experiencing discouragement. It was so bad, he was planning to take his own life.

George was trying so hard to be successful and to find fulfillment, yet somehow, he felt insignificant and inadequate—what he was doing just wasn't working. He was experiencing being stuck in life!

As you lead your life and others, you will go through situations and obstacles along the way. You will go through moments when you feel like what you are doing isn't working either. You will have moments, like George Bailey, of great discouragement.

Sometimes you may lose sight of the progress and victories. You may tend to get fuzzy in your thoughts and sight, where you can't tell the forest from the trees. This is why I believe that the Lead Through Method is so powerful, particularly this first foundational step. It helps you reassess and refocus your life so that you can maximize its potential and impact by going forward.

Like George, it's easy to get discouraged and pretend that you are happy. But pretending won't make you well. It won't accelerate you. It will have the opposite effect. It will keep you stuck in a vicious cycle. So, are you secretly discouraged? I've been there! Being discouraged is no fun. Some reasons people get discouraged are due to *unfulfilled expectations.* Your personal and professional life are interconnected. Your family relationships, finances, spiritual life, and health are all connected. Your working relationships and career satisfaction are interconnected. When you are struggling in one of these areas, you may develop a sense of unfulfillment, which leads to frustration, and then to discouragement. Unfulfilled expectations can come in the following thoughts:

> *"I thought I should be further in life by now."*
> *"I thought I was going to get the promotion at work."*
> *"I thought that by now I would have been able to buy that gift for my spouse?"*

These thoughts can go on and on.

Another reason you may get discouraged is **by comparing yourself to others.** This is especially true in this age of social media. People show the good things in their lives—the vacations, the parties, the gifts, the church size, the business profits, and the apparent successes they are having. Facebook, Instagram, and other sites are infamous for doing this! By comparing your life on social media, you are comparing your level of success based on others. *All this comparison is distracting you from what you truly have in front of you.* Comparison is hindering you from going after all the ideas and dreams that God has placed in your mind and heart.

Lastly, another reason for discouragement is that you may be **forcing things to happen out of season.** I love this ancient yet profound truth, *"As long as the earth endures, there will be seedtime and harvest time."*[2] In other words, using this farming analogy for life, there is a season for sowing (planting) and a season for reaping (harvesting, collecting, enjoying) what you have sown. Usually, it's the time in the middle that gets to us. At least, it sometimes gets to me.

SEED + TIME = HARVEST.

Many times, you won't see the results you want in your life, business, or organizations because you don't do the right things in the right order. Even if you do the right things, in the right order, you think you should see results instantly! For example, you go to the gym to begin a workout regimen, or start a meal plan, and soon get discouraged because you don't see the results you want quickly enough. Or you start disciplining yourself by budgeting your money, then get side tracked because you don't see the financial reward right away. If you are a person of faith, you pray and begin to cultivate your relationship with God. Yet, you may quickly abandon prayer and stop believing because you didn't get your prayers answered right away. If you are a salesperson, you make some cold calls and potential clients reject you. You throw your hands in the air and declare that it doesn't work! These are just some examples. Understand that regardless of the instant gratification society we live in today, here is the truth: There is always a germination phase in

whatever you are sowing in your life, both professionally and personally. Forcing things to happen at the
wrong time will almost always cause discouragement.

So, wait! What happened to George Bailey? At the
end of the movie, when George was at his wits end
and was getting ready to end it all, the angel reminded
him of who he was. At that moment, George realized
just how much he really had, just how much he had
done, and just how many people in his community
loved him. So, as you uncover and discover where you
are, be real and honest with yourself. But don't allow
where you are, or the perception of where you are,
to discourage you. Instead, let it propel you to this
new life you are embarking on—a LeadThrough life.

QUESTIONS & REFLECTION

- Where are you?

Personally + Professionally
Current REALITY

Example:

I am living in Philadelphia, PA in a small, 650 sq feet apartment. I like the area, but I need more space. My husband and I are thinking of expanding our family, but I feel frustrated and stuck because of my job. I hate it. I don't use my skills and my talents. I feel stuck in a job I hate and in an apartment I want to leave.

CHAPTER 4

DISSECT IT

"The only real mistake is the one from which we learn nothing."
John Powell

I was excited to have my brother Moises and my sister-in-law, Sabrina, spend the weekend with our family in Washington, D.C. That weekend, we had a blast and created wonderful memories. On the last day, however, as they were preparing to head home, we decided to make one more stop and pick up lunch at a burger joint. "One hundred percent grass fed beef,'" the sign proclaimed. *"Hmmm, must be good,'"* I thought, so we went in.

Prior to going to a restaurant, some people have a habit of checking on the Internet to read reviews of what other customers have said about their experiences. Good idea! But, prior to this experience, I didn't have that habit. My reviews normally came from friends, coworkers, or family. Except this day, I had none! Ignoring this, we rushed in. As soon as the waitress handed me my food, I knew this was a bad decision. The fries were soaked in grease, the bacon was hard as a rock, and the burger was tasteless. *Did they run out of salt? Was this real bacon?* We were disappointed. As we left the restaurant, my brother said, jokingly, *"Well, that was an awful in-person course huh?"* Knowing I like creating courses to help leaders' strategies, I said, *"Yup, a $52.48 course that took less than an hour and taught us where not to eat next time."* We joked about it and continued home. This experience taught me, from then on, to look for reviews! It highlighted the habits of all those friends and family that actually check for reviews. Needless to say, I have a new habit. I now check reviews!

So much has been said and written about the topic of habits. With great books such as *Atomic Habits* by James Clear, or *The 7 Habits of Highly Effective People* by Stephen R. Covey, I suffice to say that good habits are essential for success, both professionally and personally. Habits, whether done consciously or subconsciously, will determine the quality of your life. Because habits play a major role in where you end up in life, it is critical to examine the habits you have formed and will be forming. The bad news is that you may have formed some habits already in your life that are preventing you from achieving the breakthroughs you desire. Some are either helping you or hindering you. We will dissect that in this chapter. The good news is that regardless of where you are and what you discover, you have an amazing opportunity to select, build, and establish new habits—starting today. The habits you choose will determine the course of your life.

In this step of the LeadThrough Method, I want you to imagine with me that you are delving into a deep investigation of your life. As any good detective will tell you, solving a crime will be based on the evidence. Finding that evidence will require great dissecting of the facts available. In this investigation, you will question the habits that have led you to the results in your life. Doing this will require you to ask yourself about some of the thoughts, patterns, and actions that have left you feeling overwhelmed and discontented. What daily practices have helped bring you closer to the life and leadership you desire? What do you do to get the most results? What do you think about when you don't see progress? What do you do that slows your momentum?

Let's look closely at three H's in this step.

- Hurdles
- Habits
- Helpful

HURDLES

I want you to look at the hurdles that you've had to overcome to get where you are in life today. Hurdles are those difficult situations and events that are part of your story. They may have taken you out or could be used as excuses, but instead, you will use them as momentum. And finally, you will audit and reframe what has been helpful in your life to get you to where you are today. You have amazing talents, abilities, attributes, and skills that you need to identify and implement as you move forward in your breakthrough journey. What are those attitudes that have served you well? What daily practices contributed to your success? This step is what I call, "Dissect it." It is answering the question: "What has brought me here?"

I want you to become aware of how your daily actions, or lack thereof, are creating a pattern that is either helping or hurting you. You will clearly define those hurdles in your life and reframe what has been hurtful to how they can be helpful. Uncovering this, through the process of dissecting, will make all the difference from merely drifting to leading; from merely experiencing to growing; and from merely living to actually thriving.

Let's talk more about hurdles. You most likely have had your share of negative experiences that have caused pain and brought disappointment to your life. Events you wished you could forget. Experiences you think about today and cringe. I know this has been true in my life. No one gets results without some degree of hurdles. What I first want you to see in this chapter is that you should not allow those experiences to be forgotten without first reflecting, analyzing, and learning from them. For example, the burger joint was a negative experience. If I simply forgot the event or kept framing that experience in my mind as a negative one, then it would have been a waste of money and time.

But reflecting, analyzing, and learning from that experience, my learning curve increased. I call this process "dissecting your experiences." Dissecting this one bad experience taught me what can happen if I make a decision in a hurry, and how being led by my stomach instead of some research may lead me down a path that's disappointing.

What if instead of just allowing those moments to be painful memories, we can dissect them to be purposeful ones? What if we analyze those experiences instead of abandoning them? What if we reflect on the lessons we can learn, instead of resenting them? So many people go through life's hurdles never stopping to dissect those experiences, therefore leaving tremendous lessons behind. Unfortunately, they are bound to repeat the same mistakes and experience the same heartaches.

STEP 1—LOCATE IT

Using an example, let's apply this principle to someone named Billy and his finances. He is a single dad, has a full-time job, but hasn't really found the time to get his finances in order. He tries his best but can't seem to move the needle in a positive direction. He is overwhelmed with debt. Billy is experiencing a hurdle.

Stressed out, he does a little research and creates a one sheet analysis of where his money is going. He can now see his numbers. He did the hard work of identifying where he is as it relates to his personal finances. He can clearly see that he has more money going out than money coming in. Billy is at Step 1—Locate it.

STEP 2—DISSECT IT

This next step requires Billy to dig a bit deeper. He wants to solve his problem and get a breakthrough in his emotional and financial life. In order to do this, he must answer the question: "What has led me here?" Billy must now identify the root cause of what led him to where he is today. This is the key for Billy to get a breakthrough and lead his life out of debt and into financial peace. Doing this step of dissecting addresses not just the symptom but the actual problem itself.

Most people who experience what Billy experienced

would just work harder, put in more hours, and probably repeat the same actions and continue to stay in the same situation. In other words, doing the same things and expecting a different result. Yet, as you reveal the source of what got you into that situation and into that emotional state, then revelation will begin to shine some light of hope into your situation. It will give you clarity to make the adjustments necessary to change your financial life forever!

This principle applies not just to finances, but it can be applied to your spiritual life, relational life, emotional well-being, your career, health and any area that is important to you. Abandoning your faith, leaving your spouse, or quitting your job without dissecting your condition will almost always leave you disheartened, because you will always have your hurdles everywhere you go!

HABITS

Using Billy's example again, after dissecting what led him to where he was, he now knows that he got into debt by wrongly using credit cards. He made purchases because he convinced himself that he "needed" to buy that new wardrobe, or go to that expensive restaurant, or buy his kid another pair of new sneakers. Billy knew he couldn't afford it, but he rationalized it in his mind, so to the store he went. Rationalizing is now a subconscious habit for Billy. This habit has gotten him into debt, and it is making him miserable. As an observer, you can clearly see Billy's problem is not so much a lack of resources that got him into debt, but a lack of discipline that got him there.

The decisions you make are forming a habit that will either help you or hurt you. In Billy's situation, he is a single dad with a full-time job, but now he needs to determine a way to get his finances in order. He needs to create a budget so that he knows what he can and can't spend in any given month. He has to remove rationalization when it comes to spending, and to create a new habit of budgeting and making decisions based on facts rather than emotions. What would help Billy—and would help you to get unstuck and move forward—is to begin building better habits as a result of your findings during this dissecting exercise. Remember, you are after a breakthrough. For you, it might not be finances, but you can use this same principle to get a breakthrough in any area of your life, both personally and professionally.

So, now let's look at the third H in this section. You have experienced hurdles in life, things that might have slowed you down or been in the way, and yet, somehow, you led yourself through them. You discovered the habits that contribute to your success and those that have been in the way of it.

HELPFUL

Experiences dissected, analyzed, and reframed can turn those experiences into lessons that will catapult you to the best version of yourself. Let's wrap up Billy's example. Billy now realizes that he buys things quickly because he rationalizes purchases in his mind and doesn't live on a written monthly budget. After this exercise, he now has that written monthly budget. He now knows what amount of money comes in, and goes out. Billy has decided to wait one or two days, or even a week, before making a purchase, even if it's in his budget. He has decided that he will pay cash for purchases and that he will not borrow any more money. Billy has now started the journey to build habits that will lead him towards financial stability and peace. Billy is clear about the root cause of his current reality, but is using the experiences as a road map to recreate his tomorrow.

Like Billy, when you dissect your experiences, your hurdles, and your habits, and you reframe them, they can then be used to serve you instead of hurting you. You will turn negative experiences into positive lessons. You will uncover what was wrong and what was right and why. The answer to those questions will give you the lessons that will be helpful from now on. This is the process of growth. By doing this, you are refusing to just go through life—you are making sure you are growing through it. Whoever said, *"You live and you learn,"* got it partially right. The key to growing is to evaluate your experiences and be intentional about learning from them. If you don't learn from your past, you are going to repeat it. However, if you dissect and evaluate your experiences, then you have an opportunity for growth so that you can redirect your life in the direction you want to go. Most people won't ever fix their current situation, not because they aren't capable of it, but because they don't pause long enough to investigate the cause of the problem.

So, I am asking you to dissect your situation as it is today. If you desire to lead your life, you have to take ownership during this process. If you accept responsibility while you are dissecting the causes, and the decisions that you made that led you to where you are, then you can change the next decision which will, in time, change the outcomes that you are getting.

A FINAL NOTE ON THIS.

This applies if you have success as well. Applying the second principle of dissecting will guarantee more of the success you are enjoying. Applying this principle in your areas of success will bring about more success. You are simply uncovering and documenting "the secret sauce to your recipe." You can now point to it. It's no longer a mystery—you cracked the code, so to speak, in your particular situation. You now have a system you can use to generate more success.

Your current reality is telling you something about you. It is revealing what you are doing right and what you are doing wrong. Your job is to figure out what you must shift and change. My job is to help you understand that.

QUESTIONS & REFLECTION

- **What has led you here?**

- What are your hurdles?

- What have you done that got you here?

- How are you feeling emotionally?

- What are three habits you do in the morning?

- What are three things you do when you get to work or to the office?

- What are three habits you do prior to bed?

- How are these habits contributing to your success?

- How are these habits preventing you from getting where you want to be?

- What are three lessons you can learn from your hurdles?

- What can you continue to do that has given you great success?

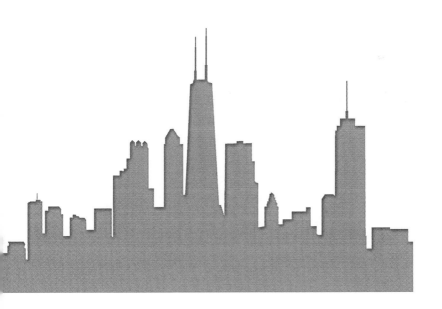

CHAPTER 5

DREAM IT

"Every dream starts off small, but one must be brave enough to pursue it until it becomes a reality."

Jose Vargas

One evening in the late 1980s, on the West Side of Chicago, a young woman was getting ready to do one of the bravest things she had ever done. This young woman was nervously taking the final steps to escape a terrible situation in her home—a situation no woman should ever be in. She kept checking to make sure her husband wasn't coming as she nervously prepared dinner. It would be the last meal she would ever cook for him in that home. She wanted to escape the horrors of her life and to pursue a dream for a better future for her four children. With tears in her eyes, she placed the food on the table. With the few dollars she had, she began to hand each of her young children out through the kitchen window to a family member. They hurried through the alley to a car waiting nearby. Finally, the young woman found the strength and courage to lift herself through that window and followed her children to that car to pursue a new life. That woman was my mom, Evelyn Amador. I was the youngest of her four children, and I wasn't even a year old when we left Chicago.

We moved close to my Puerto Rican grandparents in New Jersey. I grew up in government subsidized housing, in a neighborhood where gunshots and drug deals were the norm. It was so bad, I remember my siblings and I had to excuse ourselves as we tip-toed out of our own apartment most days because drug dealers were sitting on our porch and refused to move.

Despite those experiences, and many more traumatizing ones that I experienced, I also believe I had a wonderful childhood, and that's all because of my mother's love towards us. It was tough living in that neighborhood, but when I think about it, it could have been a lot worse had my mother stayed where we were in Chicago. My mother, tired of the beatings and mental abuse, dreamed of the possibility of a better life for herself and her children. That dream became a reality. With fear and pain in her heart, she decided to make the change. I am so glad she did.

What about you? This may not be your story, but you too may have a dream, a goal, a desire. Do you have something you want to become, to accomplish, or change, or conquer in your life and leadership? It's amazing what can happen when you begin to see the future, when you begin to envision a better tomorrow. That is what this next step is all about. You have done the hard work of identifying where you are, and you have articulated and determined what got you there. In Step 3, you will answer the question: "What do you want?" This is a question that not many people know how to answer.

STEP 3: DREAM IT.

Answer this question: "What do you want?" Particularly, "What do you want for your life, both personally and professionally?" At this point, you have written down the habits, mindsets, and circumstances, as well as the actions that got you to where you are today. But, don't stop! You can't just stay there. Getting a breakthrough and leading your life will require you to dream. I want you to dream about where you want to go and where you want to be. What do you want to have? What type of leader do you want to become? What impact do you want to have in your world? Take each question and answer it one at a time.

Answering the question, "What do I want?" will require you to believe that what is before you will be better than what is behind you. In this chapter, I will ask you to dream big! Be bold! Be brave!

Leaving Chicago wasn't easy for my mother. She loved my dad. As a matter of fact, while growing up, I never heard her complain about him. The first time I heard our story was because a family member shared it with me. As my mother dreamed for a better life and a healthier life for herself and her children, she knew she would not be able to live it out where she was. She took steps of faith in spite of fear. She believed that what was ahead for her had to be better than what she was leaving behind. That is what you will have to do as well.

DREAM BIG

Color television first burst onto the scene in the 1940s and 1950s in America[1]. It was the result of someone first dreaming it could happen. The dream kept evolving and growing into what we have today. In this step of the LeadThrough Method, I am challenging you to live your YEAR in full color! I define living in full color to mean to live feeling, experiencing, and embracing all that life is, while still seeking your full potential and purpose. The opposite is to live in the gray zone. To live in the gray zone is to drift in life, not sure of anything or doing anything meaningful with your one and only life. It means not pursuing anything in particular, but just accepting what comes your way. I am convinced that you weren't designed to live life this way. I want to challenge you, despite where you are and what has gotten you there, to dream again. *You must not allow life circumstances to drain the dreams out of you, but instead to allow them to push you forward.*

You can do it, but you will have to make intentional decisions that will lead you towards a specific outcome. This is why dreaming is so important. It focuses you to imagine something—a destination, if you will. It may be something you want to become, or the type of leader you want to be, or the impact you want to have in the world. The only reason I wasn't raised in a more horrible environment at home, experiencing terrible domestic violence, is because my mom decided to dream. She decided to see what life would look like outside of her horrible mess. And we are better because of it. You will be as well.

When I have an opportunity to coach someone, I will often ask, "*What do you want?*" Most people answer in a general way. "*I just want to be happy.*" Not to be snarky, but don't we all? At core level, we all want the same things. We want to love and be loved. If we have children, we want our children to be responsible, loving, caring people. We want to be significant. We want to be valuable to others. We want to be fulfilled and contribute to the world with our gifts and talents. Although we have all these similar desires, we are also very unique, and we all value different things. So this question must be answered in a specific way. If you are going to lead your life and those you lead with purpose, then you must truly identify what you truly want. The famous saying, *"If you aim at nothing, you will hit it every time,"* is true.

What do you want specifically in your relationships? What does a happy marriage look like to you? What do you want for your business? What do you want in the area in which you need your biggest breakthrough? Fill in the blank. I want _____.

(Examples: Connect better with the people with whom I work. To get a promotion at work. To feel loved by my spouse. To recruit the best talent.)

Doesn't that feel better? I know it does. The reason you are reading this book is because you want something more, you want to awaken the leader within you, and that is why I am asking you that question. **I want to awaken the leader within you as well.** Part of accomplishing this is asking and answering that question. *So many people go through life with just wishing. I want you to grow through life with purpose.*

Don't go through life with just wishing. Grow through it with a will—a will to go after that dream!

Regardless of the stage of life you are in, I want to give you permission to write on this new canvas. Write your dreams. Answer from within the depths of your heart. I guarantee you that when you do, it will become clearer, and you will begin the process of getting unstuck and on your way towards the growth and impact you desire. The more specific you are, the more clarity you will have to obtain what you will need for your journey ahead.

DREAM BRAVELY

When I first saw my wife, it was during a church service. I saw her in the pews singing along with the music from the band at our local church. I said to myself, while sitting a few feet away, *"That's a hot red-head!"* Although I was nervous, I proceeded to take the next steps. I asked about her. I checked her resume with everyone who knew her. It was clear and clean! Everyone spoke highly of her character and her repu-tation! That gave me more passion to pursue her, to get to know her, and ultimately marry her. Yup, she's my wife! That's what happens when you take risks and dream big, boldly and bravely.

Dreaming will always be filled with uncertainty,

but it can be exhilarating at the same time. It can be scary, because you will fail along the way. You will be disappointed, rejected often, and, at times, discouraged because things won't always go your way. I have had many of those times as well. Remember my wall climbing experience? You too may find yourself on top of a "wall" just like I found myself years ago—stuck, sick at heart, and afraid. A wall may be in the form of a decision you must make. The wall could be the job where you feel stuck, or a relationship that is stagnant in your life. There could be confusion on what to do next in your career. You will have to push fear aside and dream bravely. This process can be exciting as well. When you dream, it's like watching a video of your possible future, a future that you could begin to walk into starting today. But, of course, I am not just encouraging you to dream, I am really challenging you to plan out a course of action.

At this step, are you ready to dream bravely in the direction of what it is that you truly want. As you are reading these questions and this chapter, you may be thinking and saying to yourself, *"This is hard work."* And to that, I agree Most people just drift through life without experiencing the full color and excitement that life has to offer. Don't let it be you! You can't get to a specific destination without first being clear in what direction you should be moving in the first place.

If you want to get a breakthrough and lead your life, you have to answer the question, "What do I want?" Once you identify the dream or the vision, you will have something to aim for and you will move with purpose and meaning. You will begin to get unstuck and on the path to becoming the best leader you were created to be. **And hey, you might marry her, too!**

DREAM BOLDLY

So, what do you want? Perhaps it's a sales goal you have to reach. Maybe a debt you are tired of dragging you down, or to repair a relationship that is at the brink of divorce. Perhaps you are on the border of losing your position at work. If you want to see things change, I urge you today to write down what it is that you want. Nothing is too big. There is nothing too impossible at this stage. Write it all down. We will create a plan in a later stage in this book. I want you to focus on answering what you want. Don't focus on the " how" just yet—the "how" will kill your dream before it gets a chance to actually come true.

Look at the chair you are sitting on. That chair was someone's dream. Because they didn't listen to the voice of doubt, you are now sitting on it. As a matter of fact, you are reading this book, which was my dream; you are literally holding my dream! Isn't that great?

What's my point? ***Don't be talked out of your dream.*** Someone needs your dream, someone needs what you have to offer the world. Someone needs you to lead them. Someone needs to get their breakthrough. Putting your dream in writing is your next assignment. It will lead you towards your breakthrough.

As you write down what you want, pay attention to your feelings. Don't allow the feelings to talk you out of it. Acknowledge them. Leaders are great because they dream big, bold dreams and are brave enough to go after them while most people are sitting on the sidelines of life. Leaders achieve greatness, and because they do, they will inspire others to do the same.

QUESTIONS & REFLECTION

- What do you want?

- How do you want to feel?

- What do you see for your life and leadership in the next few months?

- What do you want for your team and organization?

- What do you want for your family?

---CHAPTER 6---

DEFINE IT

*"A leader's motive will determine his
movements and mindset."*

Jose Vargas

I was putting my sleeping bag inside a military C-17
airplane on top of a thin blue mat that I had bought
just a few days before this trip. We were an advanced
team traveling to Portsmouth on the south coast of
England, to protect the President of The United States.
I was excited to go. It was a historic trip. It was the
seventy-fifth anniversary of D-Day. A day to reflect,
commemorate, and remember the sacrifice of so many.

To be able to see many of the brave men who fought
on D-Day, June 6th, 1944, was remarkable. Because
of the nature of my job, I was able to speak to some
and help one gentleman by walking him to the nearest
restroom. I counted it an honor to be in the presence

of such brave men. *"It was the scariest thing I've ever done in my life,"* was what this hero responded to me when I asked him what it was like.

We have watched the scenes in movies of how these brave men had jumped out of boats with heavy duty gear as they were being shot at by the enemy. Many were running towards their own deaths. Many died that day in 1944, all for a righteous cause—literally, to save the world from tyranny. That was the turning point in the war.

But I would like to take this moment to highlight the boats that were used and the creator of the boats. (Dwight D. Eisenhower once credited winning World War II because of the Higgin boats.)

HISTORY OF ANDREW JACKSON HIGGINS

In the early hours of June 6th, 1944, more than 135,000 Allied troops stormed the beaches of Normandy in northern France. In spite of stiff resistance and heavy losses, the largest seaborne invasion in history prevailed, paving the way toward Nazi Germany's surrender eleven months later. This staggering logistical feat could not have succeeded without the efforts of a rough-and-tumble shipbuilder from New Orleans named Andrew Jackson Higgins.[1]

Higgins's story reveals that he had the "aggressive, self-confidence of a heavyweight champion'" as he quickly opened new plants in anticipation of the military's needs. He exhorted his workers to churn out boats as fast as possible. In the high rafters overlooking production floors, he hung huge banners that proclaimed, "*The guy who relaxes is helping the Axis!*"[2]

"*I operate in a big way and I don't give a damn about money,*" Higgins once boasted to a *Life Magazine* reporter. As Higgins Industries' production increased, the company expanded from one boatyard with fifty employees to seven plants employing more than 20,000 people.

Your motives will indeed determine your movements and your mindset, and your mindset will determine the outcomes you get in life. Your passion to obtain a goal or to accomplish a dream is intensified when you know what you want and why!

As you look at your leadership and life, knowing not only what you want is important to getting it, but also knowing the reason why you want it is probably equally important. Higgins would post pictures of Hitler in the bathroom, to remind his workers why they were there in the first place.

Knowing why you want something and why you do something is so critical to staying the course, to obtain it, or become it. Your reasons give traction to your movements and focus to your thoughts. Keeping your reasons in front of you will help you stay engaged. It will give you fuel to press on when you feel like slowing down. It will help you keep working while others are slacking. It will help you continue to dream while others are settling. Your reason for doing something is the thing that drives your passion, if not the thing that gives it to you.

I was given the opportunity to use my skills, talents, and passion to relaunch a church organization years ago. When I officially became the lead pastor of the organization, I had about eleven people who were with the church. They were the most loving, caring people that a person could lead. Some gave of their time and energy, and others gave their resources to help move the church forward. All were volunteers.

I immediately went to work implementing the method I am sharing with you. I observed where we were as a church, in every aspect of the organization. I had to ask where we were as it related to the community. Where were we financially? Where were we physically? Did we have a contract with the owners of this building? Where were we emotionally? I knew that having a new leader could be difficult, so I wanted the people to know that I was there to serve them and care for them. I also knew that I had to be intentional about connecting with each person and their families. That meant that oftentimes we were to connect beyond the structured church services. I wanted to attend funerals, to go to hospitals, and to go to their ball games. Mind you, I don't like hospitals, I don't like funerals, and I certainly didn't like sports. But my "why," my reason, was strong. I wanted to connect with these people. To serve them well, they had to trust me. With time, they were able to see my heart and my deeds. Because I had earned their trust, it meant that I also had their ears and hearts. Because of this, I was ready to share with them the first step of my LeadThrough Method—Locate It. At a meeting, I was able to paint a picture to show them where we were as an organization. It was a hard reality to share. I explained to them that we had not baptized anyone in years. We didn't have any money in the church's budget. I started at zero! Our church visibility was non-existent. We didn't even have a proper church sign! With some members of my team, we visited people in the neighborhood, and none of them knew we existed as a church! Some guests were attending on Sundays, but we had no system in place to follow up with them. If someone wanted to be a member, we had no plan on how to help them grow. I can continue to explain where our church was, but I will stop here. Needless to say, we were in a very unhealthy position.

Then, the next step was to determine what happened. I call this step *Dissect It*. In this stage, I answered the question: What has led us here? I realized that we were there because of how mismanaged the organization was prior to my arrival.

I had to show them the reality of where we were prior to showing them where we wanted to go. This was the *Dream It* stage. I outlined goals, shared the vision, and shared values on how we could influence the community. But to solidify it and make it understood, I had to convey the *Define it* stage. This step is where we answer, "Why do we want it? Why should we care?" This was a personal one, as I knew the community was in dire need of help. Marriages were in trouble, students were in danger, and people were lacking what they needed to live. Explaining the community's circumstances and why it was important for us to do something about it was the reason the church was there. This was the key to activating volunteers into an unstoppable force. We had challenges! It was a constant sharing of these reasons that kept us moving forward and helped me stay encouraged, and we were able to do amazing things in people's lives. While we were there, the attendance and the finances grew. We helped people heal and find a new source of hope. But it all started when we clarified the reason we were there.

Clarifying this question really highlights your motives and deepens your resolve. Because as you lead towards your breakthrough, you will need this reason to keep you going. So, in this chapter, I want you to keep in mind what you wanted from the last step, and now answer the question, "Why do you want this?" Answering this question requires you to be real, honest, and personal. It will give you the push you will need when the going gets tough. Darren Hardy said it best, *"If your why doesn't make you cry, it is not strong enough."*

QUESTIONS & REFLECTION

- Why do you want it?

- Why is this important to you?

- What would happen if you couldn't achieve this goal or accomplish this task?

CHAPTER 7

PLAN IT

"Suppose one of you wants to build a tower.
Won't you first sit down and estimate the cost to
see if you have enough money to complete it?"
NIV Luke 14:28

According to Wikipedia: The definition of a "plan" is typically any diagram, or list of steps, with details of timing and resources, used to achieve an objective to do something. It is commonly understood as a temporal set of intended actions through which one expects to achieve a goal.

You have done the work in previous chapters in identifying what you want in this next season of your life, both personally and professionally. You have identified the area in which you need your biggest breakthrough. This is your dream, your vision, your goal. Keep that picture in mind every step of the way as you put in motion this next step. But first, let me give you an illustration on the importance of this step.

My father-in-law loves maps. He is a very brilliant man, an engineer by trade. I can understand how this fascination for maps intrigues him. He has many book collections on maps, and if you ever take a road trip with him, forget about the digital GPS system. He is perfectly comfortable with a paper map to get to his destination. On the other hand, I have never paid much attention to maps. I didn't care for them, didn't understand them, and didn't really need them. I have Google maps or countless apps I can download to my smartphone at any given moment. But, in recent years, I found a new sense of appreciation towards maps. I still wouldn't consider myself a map guru, but understanding where I am, where I am going, and knowing how to get there is critical.

Because of my background in law enforcement, working to protect the President and other leaders, I am intrigued by world affairs. When I hear news that something is happening around our world, I now look for a map to see where that place is located. I'm not trying to convert you to love maps, but it highlights the point I want to make. If you want to get to a specific destination in any area of life, you're going to need a plan. You won't get there by accident.

Just as you would rely on the map or GPS guiding system on a road trip, you need a plan you can rely on to guide you towards your breakthrough. Anyone who has ever accomplished something worthwhile has always been intentional about the direction to go and the actions needed to be taken in order to arrive there. No one drifts to success in life. We don't drift into a successful marriage. We don't drift out of debt. We don't drift to a successful business. We don't drift into good physical health. Yet, we can drift away from these things and suddenly wake up and wonder what happened. It takes intentionality, focus, and effort to be successful. And most importantly, it takes a plan that's flexible, practical, and clear.

This plan that you will create will be a list or series of steps to complete so you can move towards your goals. These goals will ultimately move you closer to your LeadThrough life. The best way to build this plan is to write it and articulate well-defined goals.

Example:

> ### *Breakthrough: Achieve my ideal weight of 185 lbs by XX DATE.*
>
> Goal 1: Lose XX pounds by XX
> Goal 2: Daily track my eating on an App for XX of weeks

> Goal 3: Meal prep for the week- 3 meals per day
> for XX of weeks
>
> Goal 4: Exercise Monday- Friday for 30 minutes
> for XX of weeks

My example reveals a series of planned steps. At the top is your **breakthrough** moment, that area where you will be unstuck. It is that vision you have for yourself. The plan involves breaking down the actionable steps you will need to take to get you to the top of those steps and eventually hit your target.

As you create this plan, you must also consider the following: Be flexible, clear, and practical.

FLEXIBLE

Boxer legend Mike Tyson, when asked by a reporter whether he was worried about Evander Holyfield and his fight plan, answered, *"Everyone has a plan until they get punched in the mouth."* It's a funny yet true statement. Let's be real, plans don't always go accordingly. As I shared with you in earlier chapters, my plan to become a law enforcement officer was changed multiple times before I actually achieved it. Things come up. Life happens, and situations will change. This is why your plan has to be flexible. You have to be able to adjust as necessary and as often as required. Life is constantly changing, and leadership must always be fluid. Situations do happen, and plans must be changed or modified. Without a plan, you will almost certainly never achieve your breakthrough and goals, and you'll be less likely to sustain them.

CLEAR

It is stated that General George Casey said, *"Clarity and simplicity are the antidotes to complexity and uncertainty."* Your plan must not only be flexible, but it must be clear. You don't have to know all the steps or even know all the answers, but you do have to be clear on what you want and the steps to achievement. This means that you will have to put in the work. If you don't know the information, you will have to research it. At times, you will have to ask others who have been there before you. Most certainly, you will have to get out of your comfort zone in order to learn what next steps you will need to take. Knowledge brings clarity to your plan.

PRACTICAL

Now that your plan is flexible and clear, it must also be practical. You have to be able to accomplish it. What good is a plan you can't achieve? It is important that, as you create this plan and incorporate goals, you must make sure that every goal is something you can and are willing to do.

GOALS

The great visionary, artist, and dreamer, Walt Disney, said, *"A person should set his goals as early as he can and devote all his energy and talent to getting there. With enough effort, he may achieve it. Or he may find something that is even more rewarding. But in the end, no matter what the outcome, he will know he has been alive."*

Goals help you maintain your focus on your journey, but they also serve as encouragement that you're getting closer to where you desire to be. The reality is that you can have all the passion in the world, but without a plan, that passion will soon turn into frustration. Goals help you learn what you need to do to get to where you want to go. It's easy to say you want to be successful, but what does success look like for you? And what steps do you need to take in order to get there?

A well known African proverb states, *"How do you eat an elephant? One bite at a time."* That is how to achieve goals—one step at a time to take you to where you are going. I want you to ask yourself, "What small step can I take today that will get me closer to where

I want to be?" When you know what you want, your goals are the bridge to getting you there. Without goals, you are stranded on an island of desire.

People want to do better in life—to get out of debt, to grow in their relationship with God, to grow in their relationship with their spouse, or to grow their business. I often ask people, *"Okay, what do you need to do today, to get you to that place you want to go?"* Until you do this hard part of outlining the goals you have to accomplish, you won't move forward. You will go from meaningless jobs or relationships, or from church to church, or remain surrounded by debt, thus never getting your breakthrough. Let's face it. Everything good is hard! Just because you set goals doesn't mean it will be easy to obtain your desired outcome.

Let me ask you a series of questions:

- *Is your marriage worth it?*
- *Is getting out of debt worth it?*
- *Is your relationship with God worth it?*
- *Is your health worth it?*
- *Are areas in your life or business where you need to improve worth it?*
- *Is getting unstuck and becoming more productive worth it?*

EXECUTING THE PLAN

If the answer is yes, then you need to create and accomplish goals in order to get to the place you desire. It is possible. World motivational teacher Tony Robbins states, *"Setting goals is the first step in turning the invisible into the visible."* I agree with him. So how do you set goals to reach that dream that you wrote down? Of course, you can use the SMART system to achieve your goals, understanding that each goal has to be Specific, Measurable, Attainable, Realistic, and Time based. But I would like to break it down further. Every goal is accomplished by a series of small, daily actions. I call it My Daily Deposits. Let me explain.

I remember trekking to the bank as a kid with my mom. She helped me open my first checking account. I learned to understand the importance of a dollar; it was a vivid illustration as I deposited money into this account and it accumulated. When I was ready to make a purchase, I had the finances to make a withdrawal. Doing this allowed me to have some level of control. I was hooked! I began to save and carefully plan for my "expenses." It wasn't much at that age, but ever since those days, I started to build muscles in discipline for saving, delayed gratification, and goal setting. If you make deposits, you can later make withdrawals. The same is true for your life and leadership.

Daily deposits are seemingly small, insignificant actions you can do on a regular basis that will help you accomplish your goals and move you closer to your overall breakthrough.

As I identified in chapter five, people can get so overwhelmed with the magnitude of the work to obtain that dream, it may not become a reality for them. They may procrastinate or become paralyzed by fear and stay stuck in the same vicious cycle. The LeadThrough Method will help you break that cycle.

I have noticed two extremes when it comes to accomplishing your goals and leading yourself forward. Let's use the example of reading and personal growth. On one end of the spectrum, you have the leaders who haven't read since high school or college, who don't listen to podcasts or audiobooks, who don't care to find inspiration to stretch and grow. They haven't made it a habit to be intentional about their development. Instead, they chose to listen to music and jam on the way to the office or work rather than listen to an audiobook or podcast. They somehow believe that development happens automatically. These are people who are leading with yesterday's strengths. These same people are living and often leading from principles learned years ago. They tell their kids to grow, read, and reach for the moon; yet they themselves reach for the remote, watch television, or scroll through social media, always wishing for the life that others are experiencing. But, like a bicep, if you don't exercise regularly, you will lose the strength in that muscle. As in my checking account example, you can't rely on what you deposited for last month to cover this month's expenses. You can only withdraw if you have made another deposit.

You can also swing to the opposite extreme. Using our same example on growth and development, you can swing to *Infobesity*. I define this word as: the excessive consumption of information. It's a mixture of information and obesity. What's the big deal? Having too much information can paralyze you with too many options and not enough action. You run the risk of over-consuming and under-performing. These are people who are constantly reading, constantly scrolling, constantly listening to multiple podcasts at a time, aiming, aiming, aiming, but never implementing what they have been learning.

Honestly, I am a student. I love growing, I love leadership, I love information. I actually believe that we should grow as much as possible in life and be good stewards of all the opportunities God has given us. So, I am biased when I suggest you should be closer to this side of the spectrum. You should listen to voices of value that align with your values. You should listen to people that will fuel you, encourage you, motivate you, sharpen you, and fire you up. But if you are not careful, you can over consume, and like anything that is overdone, it can be unhealthy. So, what is the solution? To get from where you are to where you want to be, you have to apply one step at a time. But what should you focus on? Focus on the next small step that will help you get closer to your goal, both personally and within your leadership. Instead of going to either extreme, decide what you will do—one small step, and be committed to that small step no matter what. Again, I call those steps your Daily Deposits.

Author James N. Watkins is credited for saying, *"A river cuts through rock, not because of its power, but because of its persistence."* You must consistently commit to taking action on your plan by taking small steps towards a specific goal.

WHAT DO DAILY DEPOSITS LOOK LIKE?

I enjoy working out in the gym, but let me be honest: I don't always want to work out, but I do enjoy it and most certainly am glad every time I do. I feel better about myself mentally, emotionally, spiritually, and physically. Working out gives me more internal motivation. It helps me move confidently and ensures I stay on track towards my overall mission.

For me, there are so many benefits to working out.

For this reason, I work out five to six times a week. That's my aim, my goal. Do I always hit the mark? Absolutely not. My main objective is to stay healthy and keep a certain weight while feeling and looking great. In my fitness plan, I incorporated goals that will help me move in that direction. For example, I created goals like watching what I eat with meal prepping. I keep track of my weight. I keep my weight down and my body moving by exercising daily. At the end of a long day, I can check exercise off my Daily Deposit list, as it relates to this one area of my life. I do this for all the areas in my life that are important to me as well. Small daily actions will move me towards what I envision for each of those areas.

Example:

- Faith
- Health
- Family
- Finances
- Relationships
- Career

So, let's recap. Look at what you want, and then create a flexible, clear, and practical plan on how to accomplish what it is that you want. Incorporate goals and make intentional decisions every day that will get you closer to accomplishing those goals. Ultimately, those goals will move you towards what you want most. What can you do daily to help you move in the direction you want to go? You can use the list above to help you get started or simply focus on that particular area that you want to LeadThrough.

QUESTIONS & REFLECTION

- What is your dream? What must happen for that dream/vision/improvement to come true?

- What is one small step that you can take today to get you closer to that dream? What's another step? Write it all down!

After you have completed the above task, look at your plan and answer this question: "If this is where I want to go/or be, do these goals help me get there?" Repeat the process until you have a plan on how to get there! Then, I'll see you in the next chapter!

CHAPTER 8

PAY IT

"The will of a man is like a cart pulled by two horses: the mind and the emotions. You must get both horses moving in the same direction to move the cart."

Ancient Chinese Proverb

I've had the privilege of learning from a mentor who has added tremendous value to my life throughout the years by reading his books and listening to his talks, and participating in a live event where I was becoming certified by his company: Leadership guru John C. Maxwell. He wrote a wonderful book years ago titled, *Put Your Dream to the Test.* I have used the premise of this book as a coaching tool with leaders and organizations that I have helped train. In it, Maxwell writes about counting the cost of your dream upfront and asking yourself if you are willing to pay the price to obtain that dream. I would like to elaborate on that important step on your journey of living a LeadThrough life.

You are in the process of getting unstuck! You have confronted your current reality. Your habits and hurdles have turned into lessons. You have clarified your vision, assessed your motivations, and you are now equipped with a plan. Now let's talk about the price. You didn't think going from where you are to where you want to be was going to be free, did you? There is always a price to pay to have a LeadThrough life. You have to be willing to pay inwardly before you pay externally. If you don't commit now, you will quit along the way. In this stage, I will help you identify the price you will have to pay, the alignment you will need to have, and the commitment you will need to make towards the results you want to see.

Identify the price

You can only pay the price if you know what that price is. And, as Maxwell believes, the price will always be higher than you expected to pay. This is why many quit their journey and settle for their lives instead of becoming the leaders they were created to be. People who lead their lives towards their biggest breakthroughs and achieve their biggest results count the cost upfront. Not only must you know the price, you must be willing to pay it. This step is probably the one that is often overlooked.

Let me ask you a series of questions: *Why do many businesses fail? Why do many marriages fall apart? Why do many people start a diet or goal at the beginning of a year only to quit before the first quarter of the year?*

I believe it is because we fail to count the cost. We minimize the effort, time, energy, and dedication it will take to be successful. We also fail to realize that the price must be paid on a daily basis. Relationships in your personal and professional life must be nurtured. A business or organization must be carefully led with innovation and care. A diet plan must be customized, executed, and maintained. We must know the hard realities and the sacrifices that we will have to make upfront and then be committed to making them. That is what I mean by paying the price. We overemphasize the dream and underestimate the price we will have to pay to achieve it.

This ideology is prevalent in our media, advertisements, and marketing today. You see headlines such as "3 ways to lose weight;" "10 keys to big breaks." These statements and the people behind them are not necessarily giving you wrong information, but they are not telling you the whole story. If they did, most would not buy, subscribe, or join. Most people don't want to hear that it will take work to get the results! But you already know this—that's why you are still reading this book and working on the steps.

Jesus Christ said, *"No one builds a house without first counting the cost, lest he has to stop midway because he ran out of money."* This is the same man who built up twelve men and poured into them for three years so they would become the leaders that He envisioned. This is the same movement that has lasted for over two thousand years. This is the movement with 2.382 billion followers and counting. Do you think He knows something about counting the cost and overcoming it?

Counting the cost is simply asking yourself the following questions as it relates to what you are after:

1. What obstacles or challenges will I encounter?
2. What actions will I have to take to overcome them?
3. What is required of me to become the person I want to be?
4. What must I give up to have what I want most?

Once these questions are answered you now know the challenges you may experience, obstacles you may need to overcome, and the price you have to pay to achieve your breakthrough.

Everything that is good is hard.

Years ago, when I identified some of the dreams and goals I wanted to accomplish, I wrote down in my journal, on a single page, this statement: THE PRICE

OF MY DREAMS. Then, I wrote down everything I thought I would need for these dreams to come true. I knew it was going to cost me time, energy, passion, labor, money, growth, new skills, prayer, and the list kept going.

I was calculating the price. I was essentially asking myself if I was willing to pay for my goal, my dream. The answer has always been yes. But I also want to be realistic for you and say that the price is always higher than what you can calculate. A lot of people start and quit. They say, *"I didn't expect this,"* or, *"I didn't know it was going to be this hard,"* or, *"I didn't know it would require this much from me."* We go into relationships, goals, jobs, or businesses saying subconsciously: *"I hope this works,"* or, *"I'll give it a shot,"* or, *I'll give it one year."* We expect things to go smoothly, but we know they rarely do.

Having a LeadThrough life will require you to be bold and committed to finishing what you start. Your attitude should be as philosopher and businessman Jim Rohn used to say, *"Do it or die, but I ain't coming back."* When you are willing to pay upfront mentally, it makes it easier to pay later externally, through the decisions and actions you will have to take. Knowing the price and being willing to pay it will help you implement the plan that you developed in the last chapter. Because, in the process of implementing that plan, you will go through road bumps and detours on your way to becoming a breakthrough leader.

ALIGN THE HEART AND THE HEAD

I was on one of my walks one day and I noticed a middle-aged man and a woman walking together. They were going to cross an intersection, and the man pointed towards the left and the woman pointed straight ahead. I was too far away to be able to hear their dialogue, but it seemed as if the man was saying, *"Let's go this way."* But the woman pointed straight ahead, and as she did, I imagined she said, *"No, that way."* The man once again pointed towards the side street on the left side of the road and may have said, *"Let's go this way."* One wanted to go one way, and the other wanted to go the opposite way. As I watched this couple and envisioned what they were saying, I thought to myself that this is what I see all the time in people's lives. Like this couple, at times, we lack alignment in the direction we want to go. It reminded me of the following quote: *"Do two walk together unless they have agreed to do so?"* As you identified the price you will have to pay to have a LeadThrough life, you will have to align your heart and head towards the same direction.

Oftentimes, you are not getting the breakthroughs that you want in your careers, relationships, business, health, finances, or accomplishing your goals, because there is a disconnection between the mind and the heart. In order to accomplish your biggest goals, build the life you want, the organization you want, and the family that you want, you need both. As a matter of fact, good, solid decisions are made with both the heart and the mind. Breakthrough happens when the mind and the heart are aligned.

Head + Heart= Commitment

What does this look like on a practical level?
In a job, it can look like this:

Head says: *"This job pays the bills, but I am bored out of my mind."*
Heart says: *"I find no fulfillment doing this job. What if I could do something else? I'll quit now."*

Listening to one or the other will almost always lead you down the wrong path.

One will lead you to walk around discouraged and with apathy, while the other will push you to abandon your responsibilities.

Aligning the heart and the head is necessary to make the right decision. It could be something like this: **HEAD & HEART:** *"I find no fulfillment in my career because I don't use any of my skills or abilities that I am passionate* *about. But I am grateful I am good at my job. and it does pay my bills. I will create a two-year plan so I can serve my employer well while also creating a plan to do something about which I am truly gifted and passionate about."*

Let's look at another example:

Head says: *"I need to create a budget so that I can get out of debt and have financial peace."*

Heart says: *"But I want to buy this now; budgeting sucks."*

Or

Head says: *"I need to make this important hiring decision to advance our organization and we can afford it."*

Heart says: *"Yeah, but you can do it all. Someone else won't do it as well as you will."*

Can you hear the tension? I believe this happens to us anytime there is a disconnection. When your heart and your head are out of alignment, you will always find yourself stuck, unfulfilled, and frustrated. Like the earlier example of the couple I was observing, the head wants to go one route and the heart wants to go another. The mind is the logical one: Facts. Figures. Spreadsheets. The heart is emotional: Passion. Fulfillment. Adventurous. You have to unite the heart and the mind and lead with both in the same direction in order to get the best results.

128

Using our budget example:

It is bringing your heart (your passion, your desires, your feelings) to the table, and it is also bringing the mind (facts, spreadsheet, figures) to the table, and the dialogue could be something like this:

"Okay, I know I want to buy this home. I have a strong desire to live in this part of town. It is a beautiful home, yet the reality is that right now, in order for me to reach my other financial goals, I have to put this buying decision on hold. I have to continue to save, and when I get to XX amount towards this goal, then I can make this a reality."

It may sound crazy, but the reality is that most people are led by either the heart or the mind, instead of being informed by both. They convince themselves that the decision they are about to make is the best one possible. But what I am saying to you is that in order to make the best decision possible, so that you can get results like never before, is to use both heart and mind, passion and logic, facts and instincts to make those decisions.

BE COMMITTED TO PAYING THE PRICE

Lastly, as you identify the price and align your heart and head, you have to be committed to the process. You may be rejected by potential clients. Someone may leave your organization. People may not buy your product. At times, you will struggle to know what to do. On top of the external obstacles, you will have internal ones as well. You may get discouraged, and you may have to move and fight against fear. Anytime you are intentional about progress, you will confront challenges along the way. Progress always enlists processes. That process is different for everyone, depending on their personal journey. You will have to be committed to the process until you see your breakthrough and get the results you want.

To develop your commitment, understand the following:[1]

1. Commitment starts in the heart.
2. Commitment is tested by action.
3. Commitment opens the door for accomplishment.
4. Commitment can be measured.
5. Commitment enables you to make decisions.
6. Commitment flourishes with public accountability.

If you identify the price you will have to pay and commit to paying it, you are on your way to a Lead-Through life. You are on your way to seeing the results you want. But now, you have one final act, outlined in the next chapter. Read on.

QUESTIONS & REFLECTION

- What would you have to pay in terms of time, money, education, discipline, effort, emotions?

- What challenges and obstacles will you confront on your way to where you want to go?

- What else?

Go back and read what you wrote down in the commitment steps in the LeadThrough Method. This is your motivation. This is why you must be willing to pay this price. Understand that the price will always be higher.

CHAPTER 9

MAKE IT

"If you can't fly, then run. If you can't run, then walk. If you can't walk, then crawl, but whatever you do, you have to keep moving forward."
Martin Luther King Jr.

Y ou've done a lot of deep work to get to this point. It is tempting to look back over all of your discoveries and commitments, reflect on them, and still stay stuck right where you are. You have to apply this one final act towards your LeadThrough life. The awareness that you've received through the first few steps of the LeadThrough Method will become transformational only when you apply this final step. *You must take action.*

When I was released from the Trenton Police Academy because of my WPW, one would have thought that, upon receiving that news and diagnosis, I would have immediately had the needed surgery, recovered, and signed up for the next academy class. But I didn't. I waited two more years! As far as my dream and goal were concerned, they were placed on the backburner. Do you know what I did for two years as it related to this area in my life that I had so wanted? I waited in denial! Two years of putting this particular dream on hold, and saying to myself, *"Maybe I don't have this problem. Maybe they made a mistake."* Then, after the denial came the contemplation. I wondered and argued if this surgery was even worth it. If this dream would be worth it. But all that time, the dream kept growing, and the desire to go after it was intensifying. I had to do one thing. I had to get the surgery. I had to get it done. I had to make a decision. I had to take action. That's what you must do as well. *You must take action.*

After the surgery, my dream expanded. I no longer wanted the local police job, although I believe they are the everyday heroes. I wanted to protect the President of the United States as a Secret Service Officer, and that is what I did! You will experience obstacles and challenges as you go from where you are to where you want to be in your life. You must make a decision that will focus on the outcome you want, the results you desire, and make the change you are working towards. This is where you now become the hero in your story. This is where you take action. No one is going to lose weight for you. No one can build your organization for you. No one is going to build your dream for you. You have to build it yourself. **You have to start.** You have to move forward. You have to lead your life in the direction of your dream. But in order for this to happen, you must answer this final question: "What action will I commit to make to overcome the challenges, limitations and obstacles I am currently confronting as I move towards this important area of my life?"

There is a popular quote, *"Dream, Believe, Achieve."* It sounds good to say, but the reality is, dreaming and believing without action won't get you far. Dreaming alone won't achieve the results you want. In other words, you can identify where you are, you can even dig deeper and pull out all the wonderful lessons you've learned along the way, and you can articulate your goal or dream. You have made clear your motivations on why this is important to you. You have written a detailed plan on how you will go after it. You have even identified the obstacles and challenges you will need to overcome. But the reality is, nothing will change in your life unless you take this final step: *to take action.* You must be willing to commit to doing what you said you were going to do. Follow through on your plan.

That is what leaders do. More importantly, that is what a leader who wants to have a LeadThrough life does. That leader doesn't just wait for things to change or for circumstances to adjust. LeadThrough leaders go through obstacles, doubts, challenges, fears, and problems, and they set the foundation for better habits, better relationships, better health, and position themselves to lead others effectively. Don't focus on the limitation! Instead, focus on the possibilities!

Based on that one thing you have been working on throughout the course of this book for your personal or professional life, what is one action step you can take today to move forward towards that plan you created a few chapters ago?

I am certain that you will be better because you decided to take the next step. You will grow and become a leader worth following. You certainly won't have to put up a fake front and pretend. You will actually be leading your life towards breakthroughs and towards impact.

CONCLUSION

*"Breakthroughs will take place when
you refuse to quit on yourself."*
Jose Vargas

Following the LeadThrough Method and completing the steps intentionally towards the life you desire will guarantee that you will grow in the process. I am certain that you have discovered more about yourself and how you can lead your life to make the impact that you desire. You don't have to stay stuck, ashamed, and full of fear like I was on top of that wall so many years ago. You now have the tools and the method that will unlock your potential every time you face a hurdle, setback, or simply feel stuck. Apply the method each and every time, and you will continue to move forward living a LeadThrough life.

ONE FINAL WORD

Growing up without my biological father made me realize the importance of having one. Now that I am a father, I am intentional about being involved in the lives of our daughters, Evie and Hailey. When my oldest, Evie, started walking, my wife and I would hold her little hand as she went up and down the stairs to our apartment. It was very slow and often very wobbly. I would have to remind myself that I too was in her shoes at one time in my life. When she was two years and three months old, she started to move a little bit faster. One day, to my surprise, she was climbing up so fast and so good that, when she made it to the top of the staircase, she had a smile on her face and loudly shouted, *"Papi, we did it!"* And I said, *"Yes, we did!"*

This is what I want for you. Your breakthrough in life, both personally and professionally, is one step away. It doesn't matter how slow you started or how wobbly you have been. What matters is that you continue to climb one step at a time. Keep growing and leading your life towards the victories you desire. It starts with one decision, and you have already started that journey.

Thank you for letting me be one who walks alongside you and helps you get your breakthrough through this process. I can't wait to hear what you will create, and what kind of breakthroughs you will have as you lead yourself through it!

Like my daughter Evie, I want you to say, "*Jose, I did it*!"

I want to turn to you and say, "*Yes, you did!*"

Jose Vargas

QUESTIONS & REFLECTION

- The next step I must take is _____

- The way I will overcome obstacles and challenges is by _____

Once you take these steps, go through these questions again until you get unstuck, reach your goals, and achieve the results you desire.

NOTE FROM JOSE

If you enjoyed reading this, please leave a review on Amazon. I read every review and they help new readers discover my books.

ACKNOWLEDGEMENTS

First of all, I would like to thank my lovely redhead, Marissa Vargas, whose support and belief in me is every man's dream. To quote a Chinese proverb, "Those who drink the water must remember those who dug the well." I would like to thank every single leader who has believed in me throughout my journey—your support and encouragement has shaped me into who I am today.

I would like to thank my editor and friend Patricia Miller and editor Yasmin Gruss. You both have made this book into what it is today. Thank you for paying attention to each detail and making sure the finished product was perfect. I would like to thank Michael Williams for your creativity and vision for the layout and design of this book. I would like to thank Klassic Designs for the design of the cover; people often say, "Don't judge a book by it's cover," but we all know that is not the truth—we all judge a book by it's cover, and I want to thank you for making this book's cover great!

Lastly but not least, I want to thank you, my reader. Without you, this book would not have the impact it has and will continue to have. Thank you for believing in me to bring me along in your own life's journey.

CONNECT WITH
THE AUTHOR

Jose Vargas is a Leadership Development and Motivational Professional Speaker and coach. Jose's "why" is to awaken, empower, and equip leaders to become leaders worth following. Because of his background, he has a unique ability to connect with a wide spectrum of audiences and leaders, and he is passionate to see transformation in individuals and organizations. Jose doesn't just teach theory; he is passionate about the development of people. Jose believes everyone has the ability to change their lives, live out their unique purpose, and contribute to the world.

Jose has served as a United States Secret Service Officer where he graduated president of his class. He has served as president of a non-profit organization and led teams for over fifteen years.

Jose's unique story, experience, and perspective will

bring about insight and clarity to your life, leadership, and your organization. Learn more about having Jose speak at your next event at reachinghighernow.com

Jose is a happily married, father to two daughters and lives outside of Washington, D.C.

To learn more go to www.reachinghighernow.com

NOTES/CREDITS

CHAPTER 1—TIME TO GET UNSTUCK

1. (https://www.history.com/topics/colonial-america/william-bradford)
2. Dr. John Deloney Redefining Anxiety, (pg 2, 3)

CHAPTER 2—TAKE THE PILL

1. Bible ESV Philippians 3:13

CHAPTER 3—LOCATE IT

1. WPW-https://www.cedars-sinai.org/health-library/diseases-and-conditions/w/wolff-parkinson-white-syndrome.html
2. Genesis 8:22 New International Version "As long as the earth endures, [there will be] seedtime and harvest [time]."

CHAPTER 5—DREAM IT

1. (https://www.history.com/news/who-invented-television)

CHAPTER 6—DEFINE IT

1. HISTORY OF ANDREW JACKSON HIGGINS-https://www.washingtonpost.com/news/retropolis/wp/2017/06/06/d-days-hero-andrew-higgins-loved-bourbon-cursed-a-lot-and-built-the-boat-that-won-wwii/

2. https://www.uspto.gov/learning-and
   -resources/journeys-innovation/historical-stories
   /patented-boat-won-war

CHAPTER 8—PAY IT

1. The John Maxwell Leadership bible page 1315

Made in the USA
Monee, IL
27 September 2022

8bc873bd-55dc-4d03-9ada-0adc40cf116aR01